T0105669

WOW!
Worth Of Women
A STUDY OF EQUALITY THE BIBLE WAY

Carolyn L. Wilcox

WESTBOW
PRESS
A DIVISION OF THOMAS NELSON

WestBow Press books may be ordered through booksellers or by contacting:

WestBow Press
A Division of Thomas Nelson
1663 Liberty Drive
Bloomington, IN 47403
www.westbowpress.com
1-(866) 928-1240

Because of the dynamic nature of the Internet, any web addresses or links contained in this book may have changed since publication and may no longer be valid. The views expressed in this work are solely those of the author and do not necessarily reflect the views of the publisher, and the publisher hereby disclaims any responsibility for them.

Any people depicted in stock imagery provided by Thinkstock are models, and such images are being used for illustrative purposes only.

Certain stock imagery © Thinkstock.

ISBN: 978-1-4497-5782-3 (sc)
ISBN: 978-1-4497-5783-0 (hc)
ISBN: 978-1-4497-5781-6 (e)

Library of Congress Control Number: 2012911630

Printed in the United States of America

WestBow Press rev. date: 10/17/2012

Contents

Dedication vii
Acknowledgments ix
Prologue... xiii
Suggested Uses for This Study xvii

Part 1 Worth from God Our Father 1
    Lesson 1 The Struggle 3
    Lesson 2 Surrender 16
    Lesson 3 The Sacrifice 26

Part 2 Worth from the Holy Spirit 35
    Lesson 1 The Proclamation 37
    Lesson 2 The Proof 48
    Lesson 3 The Promise 58

Part 3 Worth From The Messiah.. 67
    Lesson 1 The Meeting.. 69
    Lesson 2 The Method 78
    Lesson 3 The Message 84

Part 4 Wrong Worth from an "Angel of Light" 95
    Lesson 1 Deceived 97
    Lesson 2 Determined.. 105
    Lesson 3 Disguised 112

Part 5 Accepting and Finding Your Worth.......................... 119
    All One In Christ... 121

Conclusion.. 127
Questions for Discussion.. 133
Bibliography.. 135

Dedication

To my granddaughters,
Cynthia, Madison,
and Baylee:
My prayer is that you become everything your
Creator made you to be for His glory.

I can do all things through Christ which strengthen me.

—Philippians 4:13 (KJV)

There is more hunger for love and appreciation in the world than for bread.

—Mother Teresa

Acknowledgments

To God be the Glory! "When your mother and father forsake you, then the Lord will take you up". (Psalm 27:10 KJV), "Christ in you (me) the hope of Glory" (Colossians 1:27b KJV). Christ the Living Word has sustained me throughout my life and gave me worth. To Him I owe my life!

I want to thank my husband, Ron, for forty-eight years of encouragement and support in following the desire and call God has put in my heart. Your willingness to help with all the household chores has been much appreciated.

In 2001 Ron and I started an incredible and unimaginable journey that has spanned ten years of visiting other countries and then living in Kenya. During those first years, I observed, heard, and tried to answer the many questions women would daily present. Their struggles, pain, fears, and frustrations—and their tremendous hope and servitude—kept me on my knees, seeking the Lord's guidance for directions and answers. Where does it start? How can I help? What do I say? He answered my prayers by giving me a series of studies right out of the Bible. They present an undeniable truth from the Word of God, including answers to the question of self-worth and our place in the Body of Christ that has plagued the Christian community too many years.

Therefore, I want to thank every woman for their example of womanhood, persistence, strength, and sacrifice. I am very humbled and reminded of my physical and spiritual weaknesses in my simple and small struggles. God, our Creator, had, has, and does have the answer that unlocks the age-old question, what is the worth of women?

To women around the world, as you study the Scriptures, may you come to understand the untapped power God has given to women to complete and complement the entire nature of God. Remove our limited, gender-based thinking, which tells the world we have a God who is inadequate or unjust and limited in power. "All things are possible with God." That is an unchangeable truth, which He has spoken to us in His Word. We can debate and disagree with fleshly opinion, but God's Word—Father, Son, and Holy Spirit—is the eternal authority. Study it, devour it, own it, live it out all for His glory! In doing so, you will fulfill Ephesians 4:15-16 (NASB).

Speaking the truth in love, we are to grow up in all aspects into Him, who is the *head,* even *Christ,* from whom the *whole* body, being *fitted* and *held together* by that which *every joint supplies,* according to the proper working of *each individual part,* causes the *growth of the body for the building up of itself in love."* (emphasis added)

Prologue

Genesis 1:1: "In the beginning God created the heavens and the earth."

Scientists are spending billions of dollars and countless hours trying to find the source of those first three words: "In the beginning." Thousands, like myself, believe in the biblical truth that : "In the beginning, God created *all* things." John 1:3 (KJV) says, "All things were made by him, and without him was not anything made that was made."

In the account of creation, Genesis chapter 1 verse 27 states, "So God created man in his own image, in the image of God created he him; male and female created he them." Jesus, in the new covenant, answers the Pharisee's question about what God created with a question: "Have you not read, that he which made them at the 'beginning' made them male and female" (Matthew 19:4 NASB). In Mark 10:6, Jesus states, "But from the 'beginning' of the creation God made them male and female."

Why did God create? Our answer comes from the twenty-four elders in the last book of the Bible: "Thou art worthy, O Lord, to receive glory and honor and power: for thou hast created all things, and for thy pleasure (or will) they are and were created" (Revelation 4:11). Past, present, and future! God's will, desire, and plan from the "beginning to end" is that all his creation can live together in harmony to exalt and worship Him our Creator. The ultimate goal is found in Revelation 21:3-5: "And I heard a great voice out of heaven saying, Behold, the tabernacle of God is with men, and he will dwell with them, and they shall be his people, and God himself shall be with them, and be their God. And God shall wipe away all tears from their eyes; and there shall be no more death, neither sorrow, nor crying, neither shall there be any more pain: for the former things are passed away. And he that sat upon the throne said, Behold, I make all things new. And he said unto me, Write: for these words are true and faithful."

Women of worth, our very nature, heart, and characteristics are revealed in these verses. How many times would we rather take the pain for our children as we wipe away their tears? God's image is in us; God's heart and desires are in us. What a gift!

So what's gone wrong? Sin, disobedience, selfishness, power, control, and rebellion to our Creator's will. Yet, because of God's love and mercy and sacrifice of His Son, God continues to work His plan to restore His people, and whosoever will believe will have true fellowship and unity with Him.

We must ask ourselves a question. Who gives the created the right or power to place degrees of worth or wisdom different than the Creator, who, in His will and pleasure, created them male and female in His own image? Romans 11:34 KJV "For who has known the mind of the Lord? or who has been his counselor".

My desire in this study is for every female to see God's image and likeness in each of us for His glory and divine plan.

Corrie ten Boom saw life very simply.
She said that God had no problems, but plans.
—Pam Rosewell, *Not I, but Christ*

Suggested Uses for This Study

This study is designed for both individual and small-group use. It encourages men and women of all ages to search the Scriptures and discover how God's Word can impact this century. By seeing the Scriptures from a balanced viewpoint, this study helps you to become aware of the great worth and love God has for us.

Many questions, doubts, and cultural *issues* will arise. Ask *God,* by His Holy Spirit, to reveal His truth through His Word always wrapped in love. Bible study references may also be helpful to keep Scriptures in their proper context. Books included in the bibliography will also be helpful.

Pray earnestly before each study that the Scriptures, through the Holy Spirit and not personal attitude, open your understanding, responsibility, and value you are to the body of Christ.

PART 1
WORTH FROM GOD
OUR FATHER

Lesson 1
The Struggle
(1 SAMUEL 1:1-8)

Call to me and I will answer you,

And I will tell you great and mighty things,

Which you do not know.

—Jeremiah 33:3 NASB

Welcome to the challenging, awe-inspiring journey of discovering your worth.

"Importance," "significant," "to esteem," "to regard," "to prize," "having meaning," "merit," or "value" are all synonyms of worth. They are words that create a fragrance of wildflowers planted on the hillsides from Genesis to Revelation. Hearing these words, what feelings are created in you?

_____

_____

With that in mind, let's look to the One who has created our mind, soul, and body from His viewpoint.

HISTORICAL SETTING

The time is approximately one thousand years before Christ was born. The tribes of Israel had once again fallen away from God. Yet from Scripture, we know God, in His great love and faithfulness, sent judges and leaders to bring them back to His way.

At this time, the political situation was like a thick black cloud of smoke, suffocating all life. The Philistines were their oppressors, causing them a painful season of trouble. The nation had degenerated into a state of lawless confusion.

In the middle of national oppression was one woman who seemed totally unconcerned but very much aware of her unworthiness as a woman.

Take a look at your nation's situation and ask yourself if there are any similarities. Explain.

_____

_____

Can you make a difference in your nation? _____

Does God have a plan? _____

Do you think God would use you or another woman as a key figure in His plan? _____

In this nation's history God had a plan and was going to use a woman to help fulfill it, though she was unaware of her significance in the destiny of her nation.

READ VERSES 1, 2

We are introduced to a family with everyday struggles of how to keep a happy family. In these two verses, we can learn a great deal about Elkanah, Peninnah, and Hannah.

How would you describe them?_____.

Now, visualize yourself at a holiday dinner party, and you are introducing your husband to your friends. "I would like you to meet my husband, Jack (Elkanah). I am his other wife." Your friends glare and do not know how to respond, but creative thoughts begin to run through their minds, including, *Oh, I wonder what the other wife is like!* Their imagination runs wild, and the atmosphere stiffens.

Unknown to them, on the other side of the room is his other wife. She is chatting with the girls as they exchange baby notes and stories of motherhood.

As the wife with no stories, how do you feel? _____

_____

_____

In many cultures today, having more than one wife is accepted, even in the church. How would you approach these two verses from a biblical perspective if you were teaching in a country that allowed multiple wives?

What Scriptures would you cite? _____

Does God approve of more than one wife, or is He simply stating facts? _____

Verse 2 gives us a family history of Elkanah and the cultural name description of his two wives. Peninnah had children, but Hannah had none. Would you agree that God has placed within most women the desire to experience motherhood? However, there are some who do not desire that experience and others who are unable to have their own children. Praise God for adoptions and the many women who serve God in many other capacities. He needs us all!

I've encountered cultures where if a woman did not give her husband a child in the first year of marriage, he could give her back to her parents. In some cases, however, the parents may not want her back. Imagine the rejection and worthlessness she must feel. As Jesus identified with sinful humanity, we must put ourselves in the shoes of these women.

But it is not like that in your culture or country, so why should you care? _____

_____

Allow me to inject a personal experience. While teaching a small group of women in one country, I was rather stunned by a question asked me by a young lady. She was struggling with her own place in society and said her church's pastor does not allow women to go and worship during their monthly time of purification. She wondered if that was right? For a moment, I thought I was in Jesus' day. But it is the twenty-first century, and I needed to help this woman find her worth from the Scriptures. How would you respond?

Have we failed in our representation and clarity of the new covenant? _____In what way(s)?

_____

_____

Hannah was not only the second wife but the one who was barren. It was a great reproach to a Jewish woman to be barren, because, some said, it was everyone's hope the Messiah would spring from her line.

Maybe you know someone who is struggling with this issue. With love and prayer, you might ask her if this has any personal significance or affects her attitude toward God. Allow her to share the struggles she faces.

READ VERSE 3

The ark of God was at Shiloh, all the males were bound by the law to go once a year, on each of the great national festivals: Passover, Pentecost and feast of tabernacles. Elkanah honored God in keeping these festivals through worship and sacrifice.

Is there someone God seems to be blessing that you struggle with, because he or she is not living in accordance to your religious standards? Pray for them, and ask the Holy Spirit to search your spirit to see His plan.

Seemingly unrelated and rather out of place, we are told that Eli the priest and his two sons, Hophni and Phinehas, were also at the temple of worship.

In a nation's struggling times, does it matter what is going on at the synagogues or churches? Can there be sin and danger at the temple? _____ Explain your thoughts. _____

_____

_____

READ VERSE 4:

Reading Deuteronomy 12:1-16 will give you a clearer understanding of how and what God required of his people. As a good man, Elkanah took his role in leading his family in worship seriously. But worship and coming before the Lord was and is an individual act. Exodus23:15b. (KJV) reads, "and none shall appear before me empty."

What does God our Father and Jesus our Redeemer require of us today? _____

How are we to come before God? _____

_____

Can we become too careless in our attitude and offerings? If so, how?

_____

What about Matthew 5:23-24? Do we practice this?

_____

Through Elkanah's offerings, we can assume he was a rich man. When he began to distribute the offerings, he started with Peninnah, her sons, and daughters.

Envision that you are Hannah, watching this. You sense the pride your husband must feel toward his wife with such a great family. Do you believe she thinks God has a great plan for her life?_____ What would be your thoughts? _____

_____

READ VERSE 5: HANNAH'S TURN TO RECEIVE HER PORTION

What are the three key elements in this verse?

1. _____
2. _____
3. _____

Now, take off your Hannah hat and stand in Peninnah's shoes. After all, she was a women, wife, and mother. What would be your response to Hannah'a portion? They have a family problem!

What? She gets a double portion to give to the Lord, but the Lord has cursed her. Why will he not accept her offering? _____

_____

Has human nature changed?_____ Competition and jealousy are the work of the s_____f_____.

Elkanah loved Hannah. Peninnah had provisions, inheritance, and his children, but she did not have his heart. Why would the Scripture say he loved Hannah but not Peninnah? _____

_____

As the story unfolds, we see two women but two different hearts. If you have ever watched *Fiddler on the Roof,* you may remember that new revelation put to a song: "He loves her, she loves him; do you love me?"

From Genesis to Revelation, God's plan has worked with impossibilities and love! See how many couples in Scripture you can name where love and miracles were the links in God's chain of events.

_____

_____

_____

His plan is the same today. God can work through

love and unity in marriage;

love and respect with children;

love and compassion with others.

Take time now to pray for each one in your group that love will grow and become the true motivation of your service to God!

Write down and memorize 1 John 5:14-15. This is a very encouraging Scripture.

_____

_____

_____

The last element in this verse is one with which we all can struggle: "The Lord had shut up her womb."

Did Hannah understand why? _____

Each one of us have struggled with the, "Why, Lord, have you not answered my prayers?" Write down one such instance in your life.

_____

I experienced the same problem as Hannah, and I had all the struggles, questions, doubts, self-examinations, and guilt that go with it. I did what was right for a follower of Christ. I married a good man, so don't I deserve a child? I received no answer. My faith and self-worth were tested by unmarried sixteen-year-olds having unwanted children people making crude remarks to my husband at work. I had to learn my—and our—worth is not within ourselves. It is a lifelong spiritual journey.

Find and pray for someone who may be struggling with self-worth and encourage her in the love and strength of Christ.

READ VERSES 6-8

Note the low points in Hannah's life. Peninnah—her adversary, enemy, rival, competition—provoked, angered, tormented, humiliated, and devalued her to worry or anger Hannah. She also wanted to remind Hannah of her worthlessness.

Why? _____

What ammunition for Peninnah! You are cursed, God has not favored you, you are bringing shame and disgrace on the family name. And on and on it goes.

READ VERSE 7

"Put yourself again in Hannah's place. Every year, year after year, you had to ride in Peninnah's van with her and her children on your special holidays of festivities. Every family member enjoyed the opportunity to "put you in your place." Would this be painful? _____Write down or share a humiliating incident after which you asked, "God, why me?

_____

We can begin to see the difference in these two women. Hannah is so overwhelmed with disgrace and dishonor, she can no longer hold back the tears, and there was no joy left to celebrate. Her deep need causes her to begin to take action, and she refused to eat. All hope seems gone, but her broken-heartedness and fasting start her on a new path.

Read verse 8 again and notice the difference between man's thinking and women's thinking. We have to read his response and questions to Hannah with empathy and a bit of humor.

Why are you crying?

Why are you not eating?

Why are you so sad and brokenhearted?

Today's women might say, he should have known her by now and accuse him of being insensitive or out of touch. However, he loved her.

Would you agree or disagree this is a problem with many relationships today?

Elkanah thought his love for Hannah was enough. I can hear someone say, "Sure, he already had children by the other wife." He thought she didn't need a child to make him love her more. He was very happy and felt his love was more than ten sons could bring her. Hannah was a woman!

Hannah is a great example of what each believing women might struggle with: (1) society, (2) family, (3) traditions, and (4) oneself.

Elkanah could not enter into her world of despair or feelings of worthlessness, nor could he begin to understand her pain!

1. This was her battle and hers alone.

2. Her needs and desires alone.

3. God was dealing with her and her alone.

As a woman of the twenty-first century, would God not choose you to further His plan because you're a woman? Can a woman feel inadequate and, therefore, attempt to live out her spiritual desires through another, or even a husband? _____

As we have started to get a more intimate look into the hearts of these two women, describe each in one word.

Peninnah _____

Hannah _____

Is there a personal need or deep hurt in your heart? Write it down and cast it upon the feet of Jesus. _____

_____

PROMISE

The Sacrifices of God are

A broken spirit:

A broken and a contrite heart,

O God, thou will not despise.

—Psalm 51:17 KJV

PRAYER

Hear, O Lord, when I cry with my voice

And be gracious to me and answer me

When you said, Seek my face, my heart said to

you, Your face, O Lord, I shall seek.

—Psalm 27:7-8 NASB

Lesson 2
Surrender
I Samuel 1:9-23

"Therefore I say unto you,
what things soever you desire,
when you pray, believe that you receive them,
and you shall have them."
Mark 11:24 (KJV)

God, our Father's worth to women is beautifully displayed through Hannah. Her example is one that can be safely followed in loving her God and living out her desires.

READ VERSES 9 AND 10

"So Hannah rose up" not in selfish pride or personal accomplishment but with inner direction and determination. While Hannah's family was enjoying the feast, she could not eat.

How was God preparing the way for her in this verse?_____

_____

Hannah's despair is described in verse 10 as, "In bitterness of soul," or greatly distressed. Therefore, she sobbed her heart out. So how did she handle her despair?

Example #1: She prayed to the Lord!

I remember hearing Joyce Meyer's statement to a group of ladies: "Go to the throne before going to the phone." Good advice! And that's what Hannah did; she prayed. Hannah acted on her own to surrender her total desperation to the Almighty God of Abraham, Isaac, and Jacob. She knelt on the steps of the temple to pray while her family headed home with happy hearts.

Would you agree or disagree that our personal relationships, complete happiness, or fulfillment cannot depend on our families, husbands, children, jobs, and so on? _____

Why? _____

Finding the right source to fill our heart's desires in our Creator's love and worth gives other relationships deeper meaning. Do you agree?

_____

Hannah was on a mission, and her mission was God's mission! Who was putting within her this strong, deep longing to stay behind and pray?

_____

Her soul heavy, Hannah came to a crossroad. With a determination of spirit, Hannah came to a complete surrender. In total humiliation of self-worth, Hannah brought to God a made-up mind. "Not another year, Lord. You are my only hope!" Do we all have to get to this place before God can use us greatly for His plan? What if she had said, "Elkanah is happy and content with me. I'll just do my duty to make him happy. After all, he doesn't understand, and he does love me?

What if she did not have her own prayer life and relationship with God?

What if she had allowed her family to stop her?

What if she had left God's plan up to Elkanah's desires and faith?

Read Verse 11

Example #2: Hannah comes to complete surrender.

She made a vow! This was not a bargaining tool with God, so we must be very careful with our words and promises, but this was an offering unto God.

Read Deuteronomy 12. This chapter describes this type of offering. Also read Numbers 30:6-8, where Elkanah could have voided her vow.

In the following Scriptures, we see the strength and character of Hannah, as well as the love, respect, and freedom in this marriage relationship.

How in this verse do we know Hannah came to complete surrender?

_____

_____

Example #3: Hannah is a woman of humility!

How many times in this one verse does she describe her position?

_____

From three different translations, write out the word she used to describe herself. _____,_____,_____

Read Matthew 23:12. Is this still true today? _____

Example #4: Hannah's clarification in prayer!

I want a son.

He will be a priest in the Levitical service all his days.

She would make him a Nazarite unto God. That is, he would be separated into God's service all the days of his life. (The sign of a Nazarite—no razor would come upon his head).

Example #5: Hannah becomes an example!

What do you see in Hannah that can serve as an example for the women of the twenty-first century? _____

_____

READ VERSES 12-14

We presume that if we can just talk to the pastor, bishop, or priest, he or she will understand our situation, give comfort, and have all the answers. Is that true? _____

Hannah was at the temple, in the presence of the priest, kneeling and praying at the steps, and crying. That should mean something, right? What did Hannah experience at the temple?

R _____, H _____,D _____

Have you ever been disappointed with someone you respected as holy?

_____

Was Hannah's answer in the place or the person? _____

Why would Eli the priest accuse her of such a behavior? _____

_____

What were the names of Eli's sons, who were also at the temple?

_____ and _____

Read 1 Samuel 2:22, and explain why you think we were introduced to the sons at the beginning. _____

_____

READ VERSES 15-18

Write three short sentences of a personal narrative about Hannah.

_____

_____

Would you trust her as a close friend? _____

Her faith and desperate need gave her boldness and enough security to speak in her own defense and explain her actions before the Priest. This brings up two key points in relationship to (A) God and (B) Hannah.

A. This was God's plan. It was God's will to use this woman, so he made Eli, the mediator in the old covenant, accessible to Hannah. Women were not allowed to approach the priest in the inner temple.

Eli's flesh, which did not always please God, responded to Hannah in rejection. God, speaking through His representative and spirit, changed his attitude. Without even knowing her request, Eli said, "Go in peace, and the God of Israel grant you your petition that you have asked of him."

After all the years of struggle, what would have been your response?

_____

B. Hannah still displayed a very grateful and humble spirit. How did this demonstrate her faith?

_____

_____

_____

God had a plan to bring His people back to himself. And this one woman, through her faith and surrender, was His instrument to accomplish His will.

Example #6: Hannah's great faith!

Just a simple word from the Old Testament priesthood and she believed it was done! Women of the twenty-first century, read Hebrews 4:14-16, 7:14-28, and 9:11-15 and rejoice!

Who is the high priest of the new covenant? _____

According to Hebrews 7:22, Jesus our High Priest has become a

G _____ of a

B _____ covenant

Could you have exercised such faith from a simple word of an earthly priest? _____

Today we can have the complete L _____ W _____ living in us.

What advice would Hannah give to the women of today?

_____

_____

_____

_____

How is your faith? Did you memorize 1 John 5:14-15? Can you write it out?

_____

_____

_____

READ VERSES 19-23

What was the result of Hannah's faith and surrender? _____

_____

Who named the boy Samuel, and why? _____

_____

Who made the decision to not go up with the family yearly? _____

_____

Who determined the time Hannah would go to the temple? _____

_____

Who was significant to the future spiritual life of her son? _____

_____

Who said, "I will bring him when weaned and leave him before the Lord forever"? _____

Who said, "Do what seems best to you, Hannah"? _____

_____

Elkanah could have voided her vow. He could have said, "You cannot take my only son from the women I love." He could have lorded over her by showing his religious authority. But Elkanah gave the best advice any husband could ever give. He told Hannah, "Only may the Lord confirm or establish His Word!" He continued to take his family up to the house of the Lord yearly!

What council and freedom! Be sure whatever you do is backed, confirmed by, and establishes the power and authority of God's Word!

Doing a scriptural search, we would find God worked His plan of salvation through couples whose relationships were built on.

      L _____

      R _____

      F _____

I will give my life to be used by God for His glory.

I should not dare, to call my soul

My own

—Elizabeth Barrett Browning

PRAYER

All to Jesus I surrender, All to Him I freely give;

I will ever love and trust Him, In His service daily live.

All to Jesus I surrender, Humbly at His feet I bow;

Worldly pleasure all forsaken, Take me Jesus, take me

Now"

—J. W. Van De Venter

Lesson 3
The Sacrifice
(1 Samuel 1:24-27; 2:11; 3:1, 19-21; 7:13)

Sacrifice, to be real, must cost;

it must hurt, it must empty us of self.

—Mother Teresa

Hannah sat holding the most precious treasure her heart and soul had longed for, dispelling all the anguish of years of past defeat. With Samuel wrapped tightly in beautiful Jewish cloth, she cuddled him ever so passionately as she felt the fulfillment while he nursed at her breasts. As she watched him, listening to every sound and capturing every precious moment, Hannah knew there would be a day when she would have to give her firstborn back to God.

Do you think Hannah ever regretted her vow? _____

READ VERSES 24-28

The day of sacrifice came, and Scripture says Hannah took the offerings of

three _____

one _____

one _____

She also took along her young child.

As she stood before Eli, she reminded him of three things.

I _____

I _____

I received my _____

Therefore, I am keeping my vow and now returning him to whom I have obtained by petition.

Hannah is empty-handed again! Did Hannah leave the temple weeping bitterly? _____ How would you feel? In your time of sacrifice, how has God sustained you?_____

_____

READ CAREFULLY AND THOUGHTFULLY CHAPTER 2:1-10

As you reflect on these verses, summarize your first emotions about what is taking place. _____

_____

_____

There are four victorious prayers (some refer to them as songs) given in the Bible by women, three in the Old Testament and one in the New Testament.

Who was the prophetess who sang after the defeat of the Egyptians (Exodus 15:20)? _____

Who was the prophetess who sang and blessed another woman for destroying Israel's enemies? Under this prophetess' leadership, Israel enjoyed peace for forty years (Judges 5:24 note). _____

However, Hannah's prayer of praise stands alone as one of the great prayers of Scripture and is as significant as the one recorded in the New Testament. "The Chaldee very properly says of this portion, 'And Hannah prayed in the spirit of prophecy.'" Clarks Commentary Vol. II, Page 209.

Contrast Hannah's deepest sentiment between 1 Samuel 1:15-16 and 2:1._____

_____

_____

_____

Hannah, in giving us an example of purity and honesty, praises four areas. They are,

Explain: My _____ rejoices in the Lord. _____

_____

My _____(strength) is exalted in the Lord.

My _____is enlarged over my enemies.

I rejoice in my _____.

In *The Applied Old Testament Commentary: Applying God's Word to Your Life*, page 209; Thomas Hales makes the following observation.

This admirable prayer excels in simplicity of composition, closeness of connection, and uniformity of sentiment: breathing the pious effusions of a devout mind, deeply impressed with a conviction of God's mercies to herself in particular, and of his providential government of the world in general: exalting the poor in spirit and abasing the rich and the arrogant; rewarding the righteous and punishing the wicked. Hannah was a prophetess of the first class.

Hannah is a woman of great worth!

Write down and memorize verses 2 and 3. Say them during your prayer time. They will exalt God,

Check our motives and speech, and give us assurance that all things are in God's control.

_____

_____

_____

READ VERSES 4-9

List and discuss the attributes and doctrinal truths found in these verses. _____

Carolyn L. Wilcox

_____

_____

_____

_____

_____

_____

Did you struggle with any of these descriptions? _____

Read Isaiah 55:8-13 and then read from that same prophet Isaiah 45:5-13, some three hundred years after Hannah's prayer. Can you see Isaiah's confirmation of God's Spirit speaking through Hannah? _____

Hannah's prophetic prayer reveals the very nature and character of God's heart, mind, justice, omnipotent power, everlasting judgment, and His present and future redemption.

READ VERSE 10

First Samuel 2:10 is one of the great verses of Scripture. Hannah is the *first* (remember that) to use the name Messiah. Quoting again from Dr. Hales,

> In the true spirit of prophecies, she describes the promised Savior of the world as a King, before there was any king in Israel; and she applied to him the remarkable epithet Messiah in Hebrew, Christ in Greek, and Anointed in English, which was adopted by David, Nathan, Ethan,

Isaiah, Daniel and the succeeding prophets of the Old Testament.

Hannah in her rejoicing had respect to someone higher than Peninnah her rival, or to the triumphs of Samuel, or even of David himself; the expressions are too magnificent to be confined to such objects. We cannot but admire that gracious dispensation of spiritual gifts to Hannah (whose name means grace) in ranking her among the prophets who should first unfold a leading title of the blessed Seed of the Women.

Great worth is given to women from God our Father, and this story is only one great example of God recognizing their value in carrying out God's plan for redemption!

PART 1: REVIEW

Read 1 Samuel 2:20-21; 3:1, 19-21; 7:13

How many sons did Hannah have? _____How many daughters? _____

What one word would you use to describe what brought her to this place of complete fulfillment? _____

What an instrument this woman was in the hands of the Lord. Her f_____ and s_____ gave God's people their first prophet and last judge. Her son anointed Israel's first king, S_____, and anointed King D_____.

Write down your heart's testimony of rejoicing in the Lord for what He has done for you. _____

_____

_____

_____

_____

_____

God's worth must begin within us!

God's worth rewards complete surrender!

Summarize how Hannah's life and God's worth toward women encourage your faith? _____

_____

_____

_____

PROMISE

The Lord is my strength and my shield:

My heart trusted in him, and I am helped:

Therefore, my heart greatly rejoices;

And with my song will I praise him."

—Psalm 28:7 KJV

PRAYER

Sweet hour of prayer! Sweet hour of Prayer!

That calls me from a world of care,

And bids me at my Father's Throne,

Make all my wants and wishes known;

In seasons of distress and grief,

My soul has often found relief,

And oft escaped the tempter's snare

By thy return, sweet hour of prayer.

—W. W. Walford

PART 2
WORTH FROM THE
HOLY SPIRIT

Lesson 1
The Proclamation
(LUKE 1:5-33)

And it shall come to pass afterward,
That I will pour out my spirit upon all flesh; And your
sons and your daughters shall prophesy, your old men shall
dream dreams, your young men shall see vision: and also upon
the handmaids in those days will I pour out of my spirit.
Joel 2:28-29 (KJV)

While living in an area of Africa where the stars, moon, or a flashlight (known to them as a torch) was the only means of light at night, I was suddenly awakened in the night by fear. I thought I had gone blind. The room was totally black. I pressed my hand against my nose—nothing, not even a shadow. In a panic, I woke my husband, yelling, "I can't see. I can't see!" Helpless, horribly terrified, and frightened don't effectively interpret my emotions in that darkness.

Darkness is an untouchable enemy. No wonder it was one of the plagues God brought on the Egyptians. "They did not see one another, nor did anyone rise from his place for three days (Exodus 10:23a NASB). Imagine!

Today, you wake to the morning news, which penetrates the air like a numbing arctic cold. In shock, you listen as the announcer says, "There will be no more churches. All preachers are silenced, all Christian media have cut off, and all biblical materials burned!" There is no voice, no word from God. We are in darkness.

Now, read again 1 Samuel 3:1: "And the Word of the Lord was precious in those days; there was no open vision." Was one woman's faith important? _____

Take a moment to stop and count the Bibles in your home. How many are there? _____

Write down your daily schedule and priorities. _____

_____

_____

_____

List who or what of the above can help in time of trouble, sickness, or death? _____

Memorize Hebrews 4:16. What is the priority here? _____

_____

I stand condemned for wasted time in my life and read daily the plaque over my desk that states, "Only one life will soon be past, only what's done for Christ will last."

Pray your personal prayer of repentance if you have not cherished His Word, and end with thanksgiving to God for His Word, His Son, and Holy Spirit.

Throughout their nation's history, the Jews had watched for the coming of their Messiah. Their years of captivity, persecution, and humiliating defeat must have seemed the longest and darkest of nights. As women, many of us face personal issues such as marriage, children, menopause, as well as living with a dreaded disease and caring for aged parents. This can seem like the longest and darkest of nights. How do we cope? Where is God? Who has the answers? We all have struggles in our life. Write down a question or doubts you are struggling with today. _____

_____

Back to the nation of Israel. For four hundred years, no prophets had appeared. So the period between Malachi, the last book of the Hebrew Scriptures, and the coming of John the Baptist in the new covenant is known as the "Silent Years."

Do you know the name of the family that rose up in defense of the desecration of the temple during the Silent Years? _____

What is the name of the Jewish holiday feast held in memory of the revolt and cleansing of the temple by Mattathias Maccabee and his five sons? _____

This history is well worth reading. Luke chapter 1 takes place approximately 1,120 years after Hannah's prophetic prayer. Luke recorded the fulfillment of Isaiah 40:3 and Malachi 3:1, as well as the birth of the Messiah as prophesied in Isaiah 9:6-7. We are also introduced to the fulfillment of Joel 2 and the gift of the Holy Spirit that can now live in each of us.

READ VERSES 5-7

As in 1 Samuel chapter 1, we are introduced to another couple. His name is _____, and her name is _____. B_____ were from a priestly family. B_____ lived righteously before God, keeping His commandments. (Remember, there had been four hundred silent years, with no voice from God.

The couple was well advanced in years. Elizabeth was barren. Her childbearing years had passed without giving her husband any children. The culture was the same as in Hannah's time, with worthlessness, disgrace, and humiliation accompanying barren women. Did this affect Zacharias' love and devotion to Elizabeth? _____

READ VERSES 8-17

As a priest, Zacharias had a yearly schedule to burn incense and offer prayers unto God at the temple while the people prayed in the outer court as was commanded by the Lord hundreds of years before under the Priesthood of Aaron. I Chronicles 24:19

From these Scriptures, can you describe the kind of man and husband Zacharias is? _____

How would you describe his relationship to his wife?_____
_____

How often do you think he prayed for her to have a child? _____

Do you think once she passed the childbearing age he stopped praying for a child? _____

Do you believe God keeps prayers in storage? _____

Years passed, and Zacharias and Elizabeth kept serving God faithfully together. Then while performing what seemed to be just another natural yearly ritual required by God, the unexpected and unnatural took place.

When have you experienced God's presence at an unexpected moment?
_____

Describe. _____

In my life, this is how God has worked most often. When I least expect it or am least prepared for a divine moment, God shows up in a powerful unexplainable presence.

What was Zacharias's immediate reaction to the presence of God's messenger? _____ and _____

The angel then proclaimed God's message: "God has heard your prayer. God is going to answer your prayer. Your wife will have a son. You are to name him John. Fear not," he will come in the Spirit and power of what great prophet? _____.

List the promises the angel gave to Zacharias about his son?

_____

_____

_____

_____

_____

Verse 15 gives a great description and key to the new covenant promise: "He shall be filled with the Holy Spirit, even from his mother's womb."

READ VERSES 18-23

Zacharias's reaction was one of _____. Do you think this would be your reaction? _____

What was the angel Gabriel's reaction to Zacharias?_____

_____

_____

Then, the angels made him mute until the child was born. Why such a severe punishment (verse 20)? _____

What really grieves God's heart the most? _____

_____

Hebrews 11:6 gives insight to the seriousness of Zacharias's reaction. Zacharias had been praying all his life for his wife, but now, because of such unlikelihood that something of that nature could occur, what did he lack? _____

_____

For more than nine months, Zacharias was unable to speak, so he could not share his experience with the multitude praying and waiting outside. His blessing was delayed!

Do we take our doubts and lack of faith as a serious sin before God today? _____

Why or why not? _____

In the twenty-first century, are we justified in condemning other sins as being greater? _____

READ VERSES 24-25

Remember, all of Israel's existence came from miraculous births. Why do you think God used this method to bring about His plan for His people and the world? _____

_____

Describe her attitude toward the Lord while she waited and hoped for a son. _____

_____

_____

The Good News Bible quotes Elizabeth in verse 25:_"He has taken away my public disgrace." In this statement, can we begin to hear her heart's hurt, humiliation, and lack of value all of these years? Yet all her years of disappointment, feeling insignificant, reproach, disgrace, and gossip deepened not destroyed her faith!

Did Elizabeth ever demonstrate doubt or fear? _____

Have you an unanswered prayer? _____

How has this affected your faith or relationship with Christ? _____

_____

_____

How can we, as women, encourage each other to increase our faith?

_____

_____

_____

Have someone in your group share a story that relates to this example.

Elizabeth's and Hannah's situation only caused them to run faster, bow lower, and cry deeper to God. They gave us wonderful examples of strength and faith.

(Job 13:15a KJV) reads, Though he slay me, yet will I trust in him."

The three Hebrews men unwavering in Daniel 3:17,18, "Even if our God does not deliver we will not bow"

In today's society of comfort, compromise, and materialism, do we *really* need to have this kind of faith? _____

READ VERSES 26-33

The greatest, most familiar proclamation repeated every year around the world, given to all of mankind, is granted to a woman named Mary, the Greek form of Miriam. List five characteristics that describe Mary.

1. _____
2. _____
3. _____
4. _____
5. _____

Gabriel tells her she is the one God has chosen to bring forth the long-awaited Messiah, the deliverer of her people. List five attributes Gabriel tell her about her son.

1. _____
2. _____
3. _____
4. _____
5. _____

And the sixth is His name Jesus, or Yeshua. What does His name mean? _____

The only two words to comfort this young woman's heart were "Fear not." Can you remember a personal situation when reason and Scripture were absent, but only "Fear not" was all you heard? _____ Fear is a great enemy that grips us all. How can we overcome fear? _____

_____

_____

As women, what would keep us from being used by God as part of His kingdom? _____

_____

_____

Are we not as pure and holy as Mary? Not as highly favored as Mary? She was truly set apart and blessed among women, but in the next study, we see another characteristic each of us must possess to be used by God.

PRAYER

Heavenly Father, You know that in me there is no good thing, so I bring to you my life that is overwhelmed with fear and confusion. Calm my spirit and deliver me from all my fears; for you O Lord, do I put my trust. Amen

Lesson 2
The Proof
(LUKE 1:34-55)

A good name is to be more desired than great
wealth, Favor is better than silver and gold.
—Proverbs 22:1 NASB

The song of the Gaither Vocal Band goes, "Greatly blessed, highly favored, imperfect but forgiven child of God, can sound rather arrogant in comparison to Mary, the Mother of Jesus."

It is wonderful to know that our heavenly Father does not measure our spiritual grace and favor by natural characteristics or personality. Isaiah reminds—or rebukes—us in 45:9b, "Will the clay say to the potter, What are you doing?" Again in 64:8, he says, "But now, O Lord, you are our Father, we are the clay, and you our potter; and all of us are the work of your hand."

I have often heard preachers, singers, and others get really excited as they claim they are highly favored. I struggled with this thought, knowing I had failed so many times. I was often unyielding to the Spirit and will of God. During my older years, I realize I spent too many years in despair because of fleshly defeats. I allowed these defeats to hinder spiritual victories, instead of allowing victory in the Spirit to conquer and control the contentment and satisfaction of my flesh.

Read 2 Corinthians 4:7. We are reminded we can be as Mary, an instrument greatly used in the hands of God. "But we have this treasure in earthen vessels, so that the surpassing greatness of the power will be of God and not from our selves." Hallelujah!

In Luke 1:34, Mary was about to experience this power. Was Mary's response one of a lack of faith or a natural, logical bewilderment? Notice what she did not say.

What will people say?

What will Joseph think?

This will disgrace my reputation.

What will happen to me now?

No, unlike Zacharias, she asked none of these questions.

In verse 35, Mary asked how things would happen. What were the answers?

The _____ will come upon you.

The _____ of the Most High will overshadow you (cover as a shadow/veil/cloud).

The Holy child born of you shall be called _____.

Can you think of other times in Scripture when God's presence was in a cloud/shadow or veil? _____

And then, after this most powerful experience and instruction was given to this young Jewish girl, we read, "Oh, yes, by the way, your cousin, your older cousin, the one that is called barren [notice the word "called"] has conceived and is in her sixth month." My emphasis of Luke 1:36. The barren one was probably Elizabeth's nickname.

Why would the angel tell her this right here?_____

_____

_____

That would have been quite the day for this young girl's mind to grasp. But did Mary question what was happening to her? _____

The angel's words in verses 36 and 37 had to encourage Mary's faith, as she had just been chosen to be the mother of Israel's Messiah. We are told in verse 37 that the angels declare to her this unchanging truth: "For with God nothing shall be impossible."

What other women in the Hebrew Scriptures were told by God's messenger these same words? _____

_____

Has God changed? Verse 38 is one of my favorites. It reveals one of the two greatest keys to Mary's spiritual character, giving us an understanding of why God chose and used her.

What one word describes her response here? S_____

Our first qualifying characteristic for being used by God. Like Hannah, she devours the message, gets up, and is on her way. It is done! "Be it unto me according to Your Word!"

Now fast-forward to the beginning ministry of John the Baptist and hear his new covenant promise given to all people about the coming Messiah. "As for me, I baptize you with water for repentance, but He who is coming after me is mightier than I, and I am not fit (worthy) to remove His scandals; (an act of honor and respect). He will baptize you with the Holy Spirit and fire" (Matthew 3:11NASB). This is the New Testament power promised to everyone who believes.

Ladies, hold on. It is time to get excited. For the *first* time in the New Testament, we are given the invitation to share in the first Holy Ghost revival, with evidence as promised by Jesus in John 14 and later in Acts, with two women in the home of Elizabeth!

Remember in verse 15, the angel promise Zacharias his son would be filled with the Holy Spirit from his mother's womb. A spirit filling that did not happen until Mary's visit._____

_____

Read again verse 35. Mary had been overshadowed or covered (as wrapped in a blanket) with the Holy Spirit, and the very power and Spirit of almighty God was living within her. When she entered the house and greeted Elizabeth, revival broke out!

Hallelujah!

What spirit do we bring into a room, our homes, or even place of worship?

Now let's read and discuss 1 Corinthians 3:16, 17 and Ephesians 4:30. I have heard it said when women who have such beauty and grace enter the room, all those around them feel an aura that ignites the atmosphere. This beauty of Elizabeth and Mary came from God, and it was living within!

Can you think of women in your life who you liked to be around because of God's Spirit in them? _____

My very old-fashioned grandmother, Hazel Westfall, who was killed in her sixties, and Corrie ten Boom were among the most beautiful women I know. Why? Not because they had the latest fashion, had all their wrinkles removed, or belonged to the YMCA. It is because both were filled with the inner beauty of the Holy Spirit. What a legacy!

What would your nickname be? Where does your beauty come from?

In *The Fragrance of Beauty,* Joyce Landorf Heatherley writes in the chapter "Fadeless Beauty of Faith and Face,"

Fear is one of the most destructive emotions in the world. It can spread from neighbor to neighbor, mate to mate, parents to children quicker that the black plaque, but so can FAITH! Beautiful faith, even tiny underdeveloped faith, can move mountains, can spread peace, can give a glimpse of hope to all whom it touches.

Lord, fill me deeply with your Holy Spirit that inflamed Elizabeth's house that day. May I possess that calming beauty of prayer given from You and speak out with love and boldness according to your Word. Amen.

On the day of Pentecost, recorded in Acts chapter 2, the evidence of the indwelling of the Holy Spirit was that they spoke in boldness about the wonderful works and words of God. These two women experienced what the early church was instructed by Christ to wait for from the Father after Christ's ascension.

In verses 42-45, we read that Elizabeth and her unborn child were now filled with the Holy Spirit, she began to boldly and loudly prophesy the work of God. Some refer to this as the first song of the New Testament. She spoke about her cousin, who had just entered her home.

Through the spirit Elizabeth begins to prophesy:

Blessed are you among _____

Blessed is the fruit of her _____

She is the mother of my _____

Words of assurance that what Mary had been told will come to

_____

Blessed is she that _____!

Another key of Mary's character that is required by God for us all is

she B_____!

Is it recorded that Elizabeth had been told previously that Mary was

with child? _____, even though Mary was a pure, young, unmarried,

Jewish girl.

Verses 41-42 (KJV) says, "Elizabeth was filled with the Holy Ghost

and speak out with a loud voice."

Attention all women and young girls! God is looking for vessels to fill

with His Holy Spirit, so we can be bold and speak out according to His

Word! Stop and take time to pray for your daughter or a friend that God

may use them in these last days to spread His Word. Make a list of names

to pray for!

READ SLOWLY AND PRAYERFULLY VERSES 46-55

These words of prophecy were spoken by a Mary filled with the Spirit

of God. They are first recorded in the New Testament as the Magnificat,

or Mary's Song of Prophesy.

Return to 1 Samuel 1:1-10 and compare the similarities of Hannah's

prophetic words. _____

_____

Take time to discuss each verse as God is revealed through two yielded women. Hannah and Mary begin by acknowledging how mighty and powerful God is and what He has done to them personally in exalting one who is so humble. A great example for our prayer life!

Both women encourage those who put their trust in God. A great example of instructions in our daily lives!

Hannah and Mary speak about the nature and character of God our Creator. A great example to remind us daily of the greatness of God! God does not see, think, or work as humans. Read Jeremiah 9:23 and 24, and list the attributes you know about God.

1. _____

2. _____

3. _____

4. _____

5. _____

Both speak of God's love to His people Israel, our fathers, seed of Abraham forever! A great example to remind us we have been adopted to share in this great heritage!

My granddaughter Baylee, who is now nine years of age, chose her favorite Bible verse at a very young age. It seemed unusual to us, but so applies here: "But we all, with unveiled face, beholding as in a mirror the glory of the Lord, are being transformed into the same image from glory to glory, just as from the Lord, the Spirit" (2 Corinthians 3:18 NASB).

I will add verse 17: "Now the Lord is the Spirit, and where the Spirit of the Lord is, there is liberty."

The Holy Spirit was with and in these two women, and they experienced great liberty to be used by God for His purpose and divine plan. Hannah and Mary spoke out under His power!

Needed in this twenty-first-century army of the Lord are women like Hannah and Mary, filled with the Holy Spirit, and willing to stand before the mirror of the Holy Spirit and say, "Be it unto me according to Thy Word."

Are you willing to be drafted?

PROMISE

But you will receive power, when the Holy Spirit has come upon you; and you shall be my witness both in Jerusalem, and in all Judea and Samaria and even to the remotest part of the earth.

—Acts 1:8 NASB

PRAYER

LORD, CHANGE ME.

Lesson 3
The Promise
(Luke 1:56-80)

So I go not knowing
I would not, if I might—
I would rather walk in the dark with God
Than go alone in the light:
I would rather walk with him by faith
Than walk alone by sight"
—Mary Gardner Brainard

For with God nothing shall be impossible.
—Luke 1:37 KJV

s a preacher's daughter growing up in a Pentecostal church, I have a library of memories of services where the term "holy rollers" would absolutely fit. Good or bad, they are cherished memories. But as a teen, I was always reluctant to invite someone to church, because I never knew what would happen. In looking back, our reputation or nickname often came *from a* display of the outward—and I can safely say many fleshly—demonstrations. I often heard adults comment, "What a good service. *T*he preacher never even got to preach*!*" Today I would ask, "Good, *h*ow? Please define? What determines the 'move of the Spirit'?"

I have come to know that many religious emotional stirrings have been wrongly labeled as Holy Spirit revivals. Like the excitement of taking our grandchildren to the fireworks on the Fourth of July, we watch in awe the grandiose display of lights in the sky, and in only seconds, we watch them fall to the ground. This has also been the situation in many "man-acclaimed" movements of God's Spirit, which quickly disappears with no residual effects. As with Elizabeth and Mary, our witness of being filled with the Holy Spirit must come from our words, reflecting the truth of God's Word in light of a surrendered life.

Read Verses 56-59

Before we take the journey home with Mary and the exciting birth of Elizabeth's son, here is a truth I want to convey.

Elizabeth spoke out under God's power.

Mary spoke out full of the very Godhead within her.

Zacharias—he is still _____

Why? Is it because of his position? _____

Is it because of gender? _____

Or is it because he _____

Do you ever wonder why spiritual blessings are happening to some people but not you? I have asked myself that question many times only to already know the answer. I am too often skeptical and sinfully cynical. These are traits I must bring to Christ daily and repent. I need to be more open to the appearance of blessings. In poorer countries, people are filled with hope and faith. My Kenyan friends pray expecting the dead to rise and their visions to be fulfilled

Has our reasoning power robbed us of childlike faith? _____

Write down a personal trait you know may hinder a greater and deeper faith relationship with Christ. _____

How long did Mary stay with Elizabeth? _____

Blessings can be found in fellowship. Verse 58 shows us an example of family and neighborhood fellowship. They heard the good news, and they rejoiced with her. They participated with them in this answered prayer.

Read Romans chapter 12, and list Paul's instructions to the body of Christ, telling us what we are to be to one another._____

_____

_____

READ VERSES 59-63

Describe what you can learn about the following from these verses:

the culture _____

the people _____

the mother _____

the father _____

the marriage relationship _____

Here, on this special day of circumcision, God through His Holy Spirit gave witness to the great worth He had for this older, barren woman named Elizabeth! In verse 60, Elizabeth again "speaks out boldly," stating her son's name. This act was generally not seen during religious ceremonies in the culture of her day.

After the ceremony, all attention is shifted to Zacharias. Once he validated Elizabeth's pronunciation that their son's name would be John, he miraculously could speak again. What a miracle! What a witness! Fear came on them all and said, "What manner of child shall this be?" Everyone who saw and heard went out and spread the news!

Now, after the delayed blessing and because Zacharias has doubted the Bible, verse 67 (KJV) tells us, "And his father Zacharias was filled with the Holy Ghost and prophesied."

READ VERSES 64-79

Hallelujah!

What a Word it is! This is a message from God to you and I. Read it carefully. It is one we should never take for granted. We should be filled with thanksgiving.

The completeness of God's plan and the equality of God is spoken through two women and one man.

Under the Holy Spirit's power, Elizabeth prophesied the work of God in M_____.

Under the Holy Spirit's power, Mary prophesied the work of God to the _____.

Now, under the Holy Spirit's power, Zacharias prophesied the work of God to all N_____.

"To give light to them that sit in darkness and in the shadow of death, to guide our feet into the way of peace" (verse 79). Amen!

PART 2 REVIEW

A.   One woman and one prayer of faith and surrender gave to Israel their first great prophet.

Who is she? _____

B.   Her husband was a good man who worshipped God. He was content with his life as it was.

What is his name?_____

C.   One woman was reproached by man but not by God. And with a lifetime of faith and surrender, she brought forth in her old age the forerunner to Messiah. She prophesied the blessings on Mary.

Who is she? _____

D.   Her husband was a godly man who loved and served God all his life. But he doubted, and the blessing of the Holy Spirit was delayed.

What is his name? _____

E.   One woman's complete faith and surrender gave the world a savior, redeemer, and future king.

Who is she? _____

F.   Her husband, a good man who loved God, did not want his future wife disgraced and was planning to send her away secretly until God intervened.

What is his name? _____

Our worth and value to God, His Kingdom, His Son, His Body the Church are not based on what?_____

But determined by what?

1. F_____

2. S_____

How have these two famous yet humble women impacted your life, and how might they do so in the future? Can we learn from them? Summarize your thoughts and then share this great worth with others in Christ!

_____

_____

_____

_____

_____

PROMISE

If you then, being evil, know how to give good gifts

unto your children: How much more shall your heavenly

Father give the Holy Spirit to them that ask?

—Luke 11:13 KJV

PRAYER

Write down your own prayer of petition to God.

_____

_____

_____

_____

Then, say in your heart, *It is done.*

PART 3
WORTH FROM
THE MESSIAH

Lesson 1
The Meeting
(John 4:1-12)

Some people complain because
God put thorns on roses
While others praise Him for putting Roses among thorns.

"For he who comes to God must believe that he is and
that he is a rewarder of those who seek him."
—Hebrews 11:6b NASB

Words are the most powerful instrument in the world and have been given to all mankind. The old, familiar, childhood rhyme "Sticks and stones may break my bones, but words will never hurt me" is such a terrible falsehood! Words like "worth," "value," "significant," *and* "respect" open doors to peace. Words like "barriers," "bars," "prejudice," "injustice," "bias," and "discrimination" build walls of war.

In Hebrews 4:15 (NASB), Scripture tell us, "For we do not have a high priest who cannot sympathize with our weakness, but one who has been tempted in all things as we are, yet without sin." The word "sympathize" in this translation immediately connects and breaks barriers. This High Priest has compassion, mercy, and can identify with my failures as we are shown in this story of the woman at the well.

READ JOHN 4:3-7

In this wonderful story, which is preached and sang about time after time, we learn and be encouraged about this woman and her culture. In Jesus' day, there was different treatment of women based on geography, wealth, education, and religion. That is why this story should open our eyes wide to the heart and ministry of Christ. We have no name for her; she is only known as "the Samaritan woman" or "Woman at the well."

What does "Samaritan" mean? _____

How does that have any influence on this story? _____

_____

Why would it be so significant about their meeting and conversation at the well? _____

_____

I recommend reading 2 Kings 17 in its entirety.

People living in Samaria wanted God's blessings and protection but didn't want to give up the worship of other gods. They mixed their religion with Jehovah God, wanting acceptance in both worlds. In the eyes of the religious Jews who lived righteously according to the Torah, or the Law of Moses, these people were viewed as heathens or unclean animals.

Religious rabbis would have considered this Samaritan woman as one bleeding from birth: contaminated, debased, stained, and worthless. Besides that, she was not only a Samaritan but was of a disreputable class among her own society. This insight into her culture will help us have empathy for her and to understand just how powerful this meeting was—and is to us today!

As we begin to travel with Jesus in the early part of His ministry, He left Judea and headed north to the area called Galilee, approximately seventy miles toward Nazareth. The most direct route from Jerusalem (in Judea) to Nazareth was the great north road through Samaria. Some very strict religious Jews would cross the Jordon River twice and take a detour to avoid contact with the Samaritans.

Traveling from North Carolina to the north in the winter, I always asked my husband if there was any other route we could take to avoid the mountains. I am uncomfortable driving them in bad weather. "Yes, a much longer one," he said.

I am guilty of going out of my way to avoid a certain neighborhood or people! But Jesus isn't. The Bible says He had to go through this undesirable section of the country. Tired, thirsty, and hungry, he stopped at the very famous and historic Jacob's well. A lone Samaritan woman was there, drawing water. Seeing her, others would have passed by. But Jesus didn't!

While working in Kenya, I felt the Bible culture come alive. For women, morning trips to fill their jugs with water is a social event. It is a time for them to visit with each other and catch up on all the latest village news. I spent a few weeks in a very dry desert area among the Turkana tribe. One day I asked one of the women if I could try and carry her jug on my head. I looked like a clown as I staggered back and forth. We all laughed, and my picture of this scene is my trophy.

Unlike the women I lived among in Kenya, the Samaritan woman was alone at the well. Maybe she came at a time when she knew other women would not be there. That way, she could avoid the women, who might have treated her badly or gossip of her lifestyle.

However, along came Jesus, a Jewish man. Not only did he speak to her—which was unheard of—He ask her to give Him a drink!

READ VERSES 8-9

Can you think of a story that makes her response to Him relevant today?_____

_____

Is class separation part of the church?_____

How? _____

Is this Christ's way? _____

How can we change it? _____

_____

Did Jesus risk His reputation in the religious community by speaking to her? _____

"Why are you, a Jew, asking me, a Samaritan, for a drink?" Can we hear her heart? "You don't need me or what I can give!"

Why would Jesus bother? After all, there were other women living in Samaria. What is Jesus trying to teach us? How sinful this woman really is? The disciples would not have stopped or taken the time. _____

_____

_____

Discuss a time you have been so busy you overlooked those close to you and missed meeting their needs. _____

_____

I think I can safely say all our hands would go up in admitting to reacting as the disciples did too often in our lives. Is there a danger of the twenty-first-century church becoming entangled in secular and organizational affairs, while overlooking the hurting and ordinary people at the well of life?

Not my Jesus! You see, the woman's first reaction was to think of her status in the religious world, knowing she was unworthy and unaccepted.

Did Jesus take the bait and give her sympathy? _____

Can you think of a time you have been pulled into a conversation or friendship where sympathy not solution was the real motive? Explain how it made you feel. _____

READ VERSES 10-11

Here we see the Master at work. He completely ignores her statement of status barriers and turns her attention toward Himself! Oh, if we could only learn this lesson and take our attention off our weaknesses, failures, and positions, and hear Jesus say, "If you knew the gift of God and who I am, you would ask of Me, and He would give you so much more!"

Place your name in this Scripture: "If _____ knew the gift of God, and who it is who says to _____, 'Give me a drink,' _____ would have asked Him, and He would have given _____ living water."

Jesus began by arousing her curiosity in a natural setting, using what is familiar to her, water. Living water (verse 11) meant flowing water used for cleansing. I get excited right here! Only living water could be used in Judaism to purify an unclean person. Do you think she knew this ritual? _____

Christ was not affected by who she was but what she could be if she knew or ask for the gift! Do our physical hang-ups, good or bad, our inabilities or abilities blind us from recognizing the gift? _____. Have you been listening to the crowd who concentrates on who you are?

_____

I could teach and read this story and never tire of its power and encouragement, as it shows the love and compassion of my Messiah! Face-to-face with Jesus, the Samaritan woman saw only from her natural eyes. She stated three impossibilities to Him. They are:

1. _____

2. _____

3. _____

If you stood face—to-face with the power that can calm the seas, the One that knows your past, present, and very thoughts, what would you ask Him?_____

_____

_____

She became more comfortable talking with this Jewish man. She asked, "Are you greater than our father Jacob who gave us this well?" Even this rejected woman had great respect for her heritage and history.

Are we living in a day when the words of man's wisdom move us more than the words and presence of Jesus our Messiah? _____

Do you know that gift? _____

Do you thirst for living water? _____

Have you ask Him for a drink lately? _____

Did you memorize 1 John 5:14-15?

Write it down. _____

_____

_____

_____

How many times is the word "know" mentioned in chapter 5 of 1 John? _____

What would you do if you knew the gift of God?

_____

_____

PROMISE

It will be worth it all
When we see Jesus;
Life's trials will seem so small,
When we see Christ,
One glimpse of His dear face,
All sorrow will erase,
So bravely run the race 'til we see Christ
Esther Kerr Rusthoi

PRAYER

Ask, and it shall be given you: seek and you shall find;
knock, and it shall be open unto you:
(Matthew 7:7 KJV)

Lesson 2
The Method
(John 4:13-18)

My soul is like a mirror in
Which the Glory of God is reflected,
But sin, however insignificant,
Covers the mirror with smoke.
—Mother Teresa

If we confess our sins, he is faithful and just to forgive
us our sins, and cleanse us from all unrighteousness"
—1 John 1:9 KJV

After graduating from high school as a good preacher's daughter I headed off to Bible college. During those years, the method of evangelism was referred to as "invasions." "Are you going on the invasion with us?" my friends would ask. As I think back, an invasion it was. We would be trained in the four spiritual laws and taught what questions to ask. Then we would invade neighborhoods, knocking on door after door. Personally, I was never comfortable with this method, but I participated nonetheless. To refuse meant you must be ashamed and your spiritual reputation weakened. Some religious organizations still practice this method, and I commend them for their dedication.

READ VERSES 13-18

By adding the above Scriptures to this study, you cannot get a greater, wiser, or more effective method than Jesus has presented to us here. This woman was drowning in personal self-sins and worthlessness.

In verse 13, how does Jesus engage her reasoning?

Then He compares waters. The water you drink will make you thirst again, and you will have to go through the lonely experience again and again. But in verse 14, He tells her about His water.

What will His water do?

1. _____

2. _____

3. _____

4._____

Having been blessed with an acidic DNA, I have started drinking alkaline water. I have a friend who sells the alkalization machine, and the testimonies she shares with me are quite amazing. Water: we cannot live without it, but is there a difference in the kind of water we drink?

_____

The health promoters, especially those who back the special machines, would say yes! Let's talk about water and use this common essential element to offer such an offer as Jesus did,

Never thirst again? An artesian well in me? If I drink this water, I will never die? He is challenging her mind with an unbelievable product!

What do you think is lacking in our witness today? _____

_____

_____

_____

What are people of other religions looking for today? _____

_____

Are we equipped to give answers to the hard, soul-searching questions thrown at us today? _____

If yes, how? _____

_____

If no, why not? _____

_____

As a woman, by the time I got to the events in verse 15, my excitement would be hard to contain. Sir, I want it! Give me this water! Sounds like a sure sale. But? Well, we overzealous believers would be so eager to save a soul we would stop and ask her to repeat the sinner's prayer. My Jesus didn't do that! He listened further and asked more questions. Why?

_____

_____

What was the problem with her response? _____

_____

John 4:16 provides us with the key to true evangelism, which is often missing in our method today! Jesus changed the direction of the conversation back to her. Why? _____

_____

_____

"Go call your husband," sounds like a logical request to me. Where did He want to take her? _____

Was this request offensive? _____

What does this request teach us, if anything, about sharing our faith?

_____

In verses 17 and 18, Jesus told the woman, "You have answered correctly." He went on to explain or expose, not condemn her lifelong journey of searching for true love and pure water. A woman with five husbands and living with a man is not exactly the kind of member we would choose to become our leading evangelist.

But Jesus had her wanting His water and knew he must take her deeper, to that place we all must go—to the bottom of the well. Why?

_____

Are we guilty of wanting the blessings of the pure water without facing our sinful life? _____

Before our Spirit can experience this spring of living water, we must deal with the sins of our ugly self. I testify that my flesh will do whatever it can to avoid the painful view of the impurity of my well. I read an article by a pastor in a popular magazine. In general, he said we no longer want to hear the words "repent," "conviction," and "guilt" from the pulpit. While that may be true, they are words we need to hear so we can deal with our sinful self.

If the woman had tried to cover or make excuses her sinful life in the face of the One who already knew, would the world be talking or singing about her today? _____

If you stood face-to-face with the Son of God, what question do you think He would ask you? _____

_____

Is there a lifestyle or attitude only Christ can uncover? _____
Can you pray the words to this old hymn?

Search me, O God, and know my heart today;

Try me, O Savior, know my thoughts, I pray:

See if there be some wicked way in me:

Cleanse me from every sin, and set me free.

—J. Edwin Orr

Lesson 3
The Message
(John 4:19-30, 39-42)

Joy can multiply itself in a heart
That overflows with love.
Mother Teresa

And you shall know the truth, and the
truth shall make you free.
—John 8:32 KJV

READ VERSES 4:19–24

Only by knowing this woman's background and the history of the Samaritans can we really understand the question she asked following Christ's complete personal description of her life. Have you ever read Scripture and said, "That means absolutely nothing to me. I just can't understand the Bible?" In a different situation, the same Scripture can bring light and inspiration to your soul. What makes the difference?

_____

_____

_____

The woman said to Jesus, "You must be a prophet to know all that about me. If you are, I have a question. Tell me, Sir, where are people to go to worship? Jerusalem? Mt. Gerizim?"

Can you sense her spiritual understanding begin to open by her question? _____

What would be your answer to that question and why? _____

_____

_____

After this deep, revealing exchange with a Jewish man, who she recognized as a prophet, she has the freedom to ask a religious question. Why would she ask such a question, and why did it matter? _____

_____

Have you ever been asked which church is right or which Bible is true?

_____

How do you know your faith or religion is the right one? _____

Does it really matter anyway? _____

All are good questions that require an answer.

This Samaritan woman was not worthy or allowed to enter the temple at Jerusalem. "Righteous Jews" rejected Samaritans. Because many spiritual experiences took place at Mt. Gerizim, they made it their place of worship. However, God had commanded Jerusalem to be set apart for sacrifice, atonement, and His Holy Presence.

It is interesting that after this brief conversation with this Jewish man she believes to be holy, she wanted to know where to worship. Spiritual desires had been aroused within her, but she was banned from God's temple in Jerusalem.

New technology makes it possible for us to be bombarded daily by messages of visual prosperous success. How would you answer a soul looking for a place to worship? Discuss without promoting an organization or a labeled denomination.

_____

_____

_____

Exciting, energized, professional singing is different than worship. Explain the difference. _____

_____

_____

READ VERSES 21-24

Imagine the Great Wall of China and what would happen if one man led a group of people to take hammers and begin to break down this great wall. Yet, what Jesus was establishing here for the first time and to a woman was breaking down strong religious walls that separated peoples. Ephesians 2:14.

"Not in Jerusalem! Not in Mt Gerizim! Not any present or future man-made temple can you worship the Father." Only in spirit and truth! These are powerful words to ponder!

In verse 22, Jesus told the woman, "You worship what you do not know." Explain what seem to be harsh words to her. _____

_____

_____

_____

_____

Give examples of how His words can be relevant today? _____

_____

_____

_____

Jesus challenged the mind and spiritual heart of a *woman*. One unworthy to enter the inner sanctuary with God's Holy Presence was set free from a life sentence of bondage to come before God in worship! *Hallelujah!*

Verse 24 (KJV) is unchangeable, unmovable, undisputed Word of God: "God is a Spirit: and they that worship him must worship him in spirit and in truth." Only in spirit and truth!

A long time ago, I heard a statement that went something like this: "A spirit without truth can be dangerous, and truth without spirit is ineffective."

Explain what Jesus said to this Samaritan woman means to women today? _____

Jesus' declaration of the truth and gospel of the new covenant broke down centuries of religious rituals. Have we again built up partitions?

———————————————

READ VERSES 25-26

In verse 25, we read about a rejected woman who knew her Hebrew Scriptures. She reminded Him that all of this will take place when the Messiah, the Anointed One, comes. We will all be set free when He comes! The Messiah will tell us all things.!

When He comes!

Read verse 26 and shout hallelujah! Shout it again! Hallelujah! For the *first* time in Christ's ministry, He openly declared himself, "The Messiah has come. I am He." And He told it to a woman.

Excuse my excitement, but I get passionate and thrilled with the Word of God as He has revealed that freedom to me, along with love and compassion! Praise the Lord!

READ VERSES 27-29

One face-to-face interview with Jesus, the Messiah, and we have the first evangelist of the new covenant with converts! You guessed it; it was a _____!

Ephesian 2:14-22 (NASB) reads, "For He Himself is our peace, who made both groups into one [Jews and Gentiles] and broke down the barrier of the dividing wall." Did he mean only men? _____

The Samaritan woman was restored, forgiven, and made new by Christ Himself!

Knowing the disciples would be uncomfortable, she headed back to her city and began to preach and preach to the men of the city! The very ones she thought would bring her true love, self-worth. Her message? I'm listening as a woman.

Come see a man who told me everything I've done.

Come see a man who said I can worship anywhere.

Come see a man who did not want me for my body.

Come see a man who did not condemn me.

Come see a man who is a Jew and talked to me.

Come see a man who treats me with respect.

Come see a man who gave me worth and value!

Is not this the Christ? You've got to meet him!

The lowly is once again exalted!

Have you met the Messiah? If so., was that meeting so freeing and cleansing that you just had to tell your friends they had to meet Him and that you are free? If not, hear this woman's words and follow her example with repentance and belief, and you will experience great peace, freedom, and worth!

Write down your testimony and then read it back to yourself. Would you be convinced you had met the Savior of the world? _____

_____

_____

READ VERSES 39-42

What a preacher she must have been! Many believed He, the Messiah, had come just from her testimony! What passion and inspiration she must have had to make them believe and want to meet Him for themselves. That's evangelism! Though it is great to share your pastor's or friends' testimonies, the truly effective witness is yours and your appointment with the Messiah.

What a legacy this sinful, rejected, worthless to society woman at the well had to her credit. Many listened, and many from the city met Him and believed! Would she be invited to your church?

"I've just seen Jesus, I tell you He's alive." That was her song to her world!

Jesus has liberated women and all mankind and lifted them to equality, a system unknown in first century Palestine. "For in Him we live, and move, and have our being" (Acts 17:28a).

PART 3 REVIEW

List the reasons the woman at the well became the first effective evangelist to bring men and women to Christ.

1. _____

2. _____

3. _____

4. _____

PROMISE

Pass me not Oh, Gentle Savior,

Hear my humble cry,

While on others

Thou art calling, do not

Pass me by.

Fanny J. Crosby

PRAYER

Give her of the fruit of her hands; and let her

own works praise her in the gates

—Proverbs 31:31 KJV

Write out your prayer of thanksgiving for the Messiah's living water.

_____

_____

_____

_____

_____

_____

PART 4
WRONG WORTH FROM
AN "ANGEL OF LIGHT"

Lesson 1
Deceived

(GENESIS 3:1-7)

A false witness will not go unpunished, and

he who tells lies will not escape.

—Proverbs 19:5 NASB

Anyone remember the commercial by Cybil Shepherd for L'Oreal hair color? At the end of the commercial in a very smooth, sexy, self-confident voice, she says, "I'm worth it."

I can also remember a large billboard with a woman seated, one leg propped up like a man would, and a cigarette in hand. She displayed such freedom, strength, and boldness as she declared to the women's world, "We've come a long way, baby." And so we have—or have we?

Forgive me for mentioning my grandmother again, but her life testimony has great impact. She was a Methodist filled with the Holy

Spirit, bold in Bible truth, and strong in her convictions. One of her great passions was standing against alcohol and how it destroys lives, families, and community. She witnessed this close up.

My grandpa would drive her to every revival in town, and the denominational label was not important. One night on their way home from a revival meeting, traveling about twenty-five miles an hour in their old car, a man leaving a tavern crossed the center line and hit them head-on. My grandmother died instantly, and my grandfather died a week later. Her testimony was verified by their death.

As a woman of her time, my grandmother did not have many rights or the opportunity to fulfill her heart's desire and spiritual call. So she graciously served her neighborhood as a layperson. Though my grandparents were poor, they did what they could to server those with even less. The mayor attended her funeral and said, "Here lies the mainstay of our community."

I've asked myself, *How far have we come?* Women's lib, aggression, self-assertion, confidence, rights, breaking the glass ceiling. Hoorah!

Don't get me wrong. I am passionate about equality but not as the world presents it. I am passionate about equality as Christ has given to all!

Are Satan's kingdom and Christ's kingdom being blurred? I firmly believe one of the major causes of abuse, violence, AIDS, fatherless children, even tribalism—especially in third world countries and the United States—is that we do not see each other through God's eyes. We do not see each other as He sees His children. I also firmly believe the church, Christ's followers, should lead by being an example to the world. But are we? _____

Romans 2:11 says, "For there is no respect of persons with God."

"But I fear [or afraid]," said Paul in 2 Corinthians 11:3, 4 (NASB), "that, as the serpent deceived Eve by his craftiness, your minds will be led astray from the simplicity and purity of devotion to Christ. For if one comes and preaches another Jesus whom we have not preached, or you receive a different spirit which you have not received, or a different gospel which you have not accepted, you bear this beautifully."

Was he speaking to women only? _____

Was he warning them about a weakness in Eve or Satan's subtle, powerful deception? _____

READ GENESIS 3:1-7

Accusation, speculation, blame, and weakness have all been used to establish women's lesser value and male dominance. Yet Eve, God's first created female, must have encompassed all the grace, beauty, and uniqueness of the Creator. Eve, the topic of many jokes, can blind us from seeing the real danger and power in this.

In Revelation 12;9, John described the Serpent as the great dragon, the Devil. Satan was more subtle/crafty and wise than any beast God had made. Now here's something that doesn't make sense to me. If you wanted to take over God's position, as we read in Isaiah 14, and stop the creative process of God's plan and prove you are as powerful and mighty as God, would you attack the weaker vessel—in this case, Eve? That would not prove your strength, wisdom, or craftiness. But to come face-to-face with beauty, power, and influence—the one creation that births the plan and Son of God, your enemy—and deceive them, you can claim victory, and the war begins!

What reasons have you heard for the Serpent to have come to Eve?

_____

_____

Eve had no competition.

Eve had no worries about "the other women."

Eve stood side by side with Adam.

Eve had equal power in ruling all God's created world.

Eve was one flesh with Adam.

Eve was created in God's image.

Eve is the mother of all living.

Eve was the first creation of mankind made to populate God's new earth.

Why wouldn't the Serpent tempt her first?

I heard someone say the first woman came from man, and since then, every man has come from women. Quite the thought! God loves equality!

Compare the methods. At the beginning of the conversation Jesus has with the woman at the well, He directs the woman's attention away from herself and toward Him.

Here in this first encounter with the Serpent, he does what?

1. Instills _____

2. Changes or contradicts _____

3. He concentrates or manipulates her thinking toward whom?

_____

If you were presented with an offer that

Your e_____will see clearer.

You w_____be like God The KJV translates God with a small g and an s to create a plural. Something to think about in our day of diversity.

You w_____have w_____to know good and evil.

You w_____have confidence, power, worth, pride and can have it a_____.

How would you react? _____

What is usually the first part of our beautiful bodies that starts us on the road to deception? _____

"And the woman _____."

1. Tree was _____, satisfy my flesh/

2. Tree l_____, beautiful to have.

3. Tree will make me _____! Feel good about myself.

4. She wanted m_____of everything from this tree that she had been given from God, her Creator. Satan knows how to sow discontentment in women!

Satan transforms himself into what? _____

_____

Satan's ministers are also transformed into what? _____

_____

What represents righteousness to deceive the world? _____

_____

No, the world is already his, and he rules not with equality but with greed, power, dominance, oppression, and deception!

What is the strategy to deceive? _____

READ 1 JOHN 2:15-17

1. Lust of the _____, I want.

2. Lust of the _____, I see.

3. Pride of _____, I deserve it; I can become it.

Everything offered to Eve in the garden!

List ways Satan deceives women today.

_____

_____

_____

_____

What can we use to combat the deceiver, Satan? _____

_____

Jesus gives us the answer in His encounter with the Devil. What was

his weapon? _____

What mistakes did Eve make in the garden with the Serpent? _____

_____

_____

How can we identify an "angel of light" empowered by Satan? _____

_____

_____

"But I fear" lest our worth has been given us from an angel of light!

Carolyn L. Wilcox

PROMISE

No temptation has overtaken you but such as is common to man; And God is faithful, who will not allow you to be tempted beyond what you are able, but with the temptation will provide the way to escape also, so that you will be able to endure it.
—1 Corinthians 10:13 (NASB)

PRAYER

Our Father who is in heaven,

Hallowed be your name

Your kingdom come,

Your will be done, On earth as it is in heaven.

Give us this day our daily bread,

And forgive us our debts, as we also forgive our debtors

And do not lead us into temptation, but deliver us from evil.

For Yours is the kingdom and the power and the glory forever.

Amen.

—The Lord's Prayer (emphasis mine)

Lesson 2
Determined

(SCRIPTURE: 1 KINGS 21:1-16, 23-25;
HISTORY: 1 KINGS 16:29-33)

It is better to live in the wilderness, than with

a contentious and an angry woman.

—Proverbs 21:19 KJV

"You are not going to dress and look like Jezebel," I was told as a young girl. So my impression of Jezebel was of a woman who wore makeup and worked the street corners. What comes to your mind when you hear the name Jezebel?_____

_____

My description of a Jezebel was not exactly the one of the Bible. Many women in the Hebrew Scriptures had little personal identity and were often pawns in the hands of men for their own personal or political use. Sad to say this remains the situation in too many parts of our world. I would like to be able to say not in the church or the Christian world, but abuse and oppression are still alive and well!

Not so with Jezebel, she was the daughter of Ethbaal, the king of Sidon. Royalty, power, and self-confidence were in her bloodline. Jezebel was a powerful political figure! In today's world, she might be seen as a successful leader.

Would you feel complimented to be called a Jezebel? _____

Nonetheless, as women, we may have more in common with her than we would like to think.

READ 1 KINGS 16:30-31

Ahab was the seventh king of Israel. Two key elements of his reigning legacy are:

_____. But even worse than that, he _____and her name was? _____

What a reputation for a couple!

Was my mother-in-law pleased when I married her son? Was God pleased? Are you praying for your sons and daughters to find a believing mate while young and according to the will of God? That is a mother's heart.

A woman's influence, faith, and character set the atmosphere of a home. Do you agree or disagree? _____

Why? _____

Jezebel brought into this marriage relationship her religion and worship of Baal from her homeland. Did that influence the nation of Israel?

_____

What about our nation? Can one woman make a difference? _____

Will my God, beliefs, or practices impact my family, neighbors, or nation? _____

How? _____

1 Kings 18:4a kjv:
"For it was so, when Jezebel cut off the prophets of the Lord",

In getting acquainted with Jezebel, we discover the first key to her character. She was determined to exalt her gods and replace the God of Israel. She worshipped Baal—or lord of the fly—an idol of a supreme male god of the Phoenicians and Canaanites. This worship among the Jews included elaborate pomp and rituals.

Jezebel used her power, position, and sexuality to carry out her desires and build temples with altars as she directed. People feared her political power, as shown when she ordered the destruction of the prophets of the Lord. Determined, dominating, and demanding described Jezebel and gave her power and prominence.

Remember what the Serpent promised Eve? You shall be as _____

READ 1 KINGS 21:1-16

As you read this story, discuss the characteristics and relationship of Jezebel and her husband, King Ahab, and how their examples are relevant today. I list some here.

> Ahab was greedy and coveted what did not belong to him.
>
> The vineyard next to his palace belonged to Naboth, and his inheritance was commanded by God not to be sold (Leviticus 25:23).
>
> Ahab, acting like a spoiled child, pouted and would not eat.
>
> Jezebel was determined they would get it and stepped in with her womanly influence, saying, "Are you not the king of Israel? Get up and take charge!"

Have you ever given wrong counsel when fighting for your rights? _____

I am guilty!

Jezebel, determined to get her way, took authority that was not given her to write a letter in her husband's name, using the people to set a trap for Naboth. She used her power, sexuality, goals and desires, and determination to satisfy and appease her fleshly, sinful self. Why? Because she could. She was the queen.

Can Christian women be guilty of these traits? _____

Where do they come from? _____

Lust of the eyes, lust of the flesh, and pride of life are serious temptations facing the women of the twenty-first century. The angel of light wants to convince our minds it is about us. Feel good about myself, I am worth it, I deserve it, I have rights!

Is success wrong? _____

Is beauty wrong? _____

Is goal-setting wrong? _____

Is determination wrong? _____

Is leadership wrong in the body of Christ? _____

If the above is for our desires, lust, power, and at the expense of others, the answer to all the above is yes. Do you agree or disagree? _____

Why?_____

As Christian women, how can we be successful and know the difference? _____

_____

Jezebel—determined, strong, self-willed, dominant, exploitative, forceful, selfish, crafty, self-serving, self-confident, and self-assured—can easily be camouflaged as the only way to succeed. But in which world?

_____

Have the two worlds become pureed? _____

READ 1 KINGS 21:23-25

"There was none like unto Ahab who sold himself to do evil in the sight of the Lord, whom Jezebel his wife incited [stirred up]."

Could all of Jezebel's abilities and characteristics been used for God's purpose? _____

Are strong leadership characteristics sinful? _____

Does being a servant mean abuse or misuse by others? _____

No voice, no power, no rights: is this God's worth for women? _____

Is possessing Jezebel's characteristics acceptable for Christian men? _____

Knowing and understanding the difference in today's world is very important for the believer. "The heart is deceitful above all things, and desperately wicked: who can know it?" (Jeremiah 17:9).

Read about Jezebel's end in 2 Kings 9:30-37, and see the results of a selfish life. God has a standard, and it is the highest one can attain!

PROMISE

The memory of the righteous

Is blessed,

But the name of the wicked will rot.

—Proverbs 10:7 NASB

PRAYER

Dear Lord, I acknowledge that all my

Gifts, abilities and womanhood is from you,

Take me mind, body and soul for your plan and purpose.

Under your wisdom and word help me obtain my potential

to stand before you and hear, well done, good and

faithful servant enter into the joys of the Lord.

Amen.

Lesson 3
Disguised

(2 Corinthians 11:13-15; 1 John 2:15-17, 28, 29; 3:1-2)

No one can serve two masters; for either he will hate the one and love the other, or he will hold to one and despise the other.

Matthew 6:24 NASB

I recall newspaper articles expressing concern when we were introduced to Dolly, the cloned sheep. "We are playing God; it is wrong," was the outrage.

I had a friend whose husband would buy her expensive jewelry, and to make sure I didn't mistake it as costume jewelry, she always informed me of the price. Quite frankly, that was the only way I would know. As a preacher's daughter, jewelry was considered "worldly adornment" back then, so I never made it my business to be a jewelry inspector.

The Bible states that Satan transforms or disguises himself into something he is not—an angel of light—and his ministers preach righteousness.

Halloween is a time for masquerade parties. The Christian world warns us of the evil of witches and demons, and tells us we should not take part in such parties, and rightfully so. However, while we are concerned about the masquerade parties, Satan is sitting in the pews, pulpits, and choir dressed acceptably for the occasion as an angel of light.

Have we been subtly deceived? _____

What has happened to the church world today? Are we required to be cloned like Barbie dolls that never age and project it as God is blessing? Flaunting our ageless bodies leaves the impression other women have fallen short. If we do it "their" way, will God bless us, too?

Who are we exalting these days? _____

Oh, "We have come a long way, baby," but who is directing the way?

How many would like to stand before God with the record of Mother Teresa? Who of us would not want Mother Teresa's record while looking like Princess Diana _____

As followers of Christ, we must be careful not to give a false image or a false gospel. Lust of the eyes, lust of the flesh, and pride of life are in Satan's arena of false worth.

I enjoy using show-and-tell when teaching, especially in another country, for it helps greatly in understanding the message. Once I used a demonstration to teach a large group of women representing seven different language dialects. Needless to say, I needed total reliance on God's Spirit to do the teaching. I put on a pair of old, battered shoes and an oversized, well-worn, drab dress to be introduced as the day's dynamic speaker. My embarrassment and their shock were priceless. I did a simple change. I put on a very colorful shawl and pushed my feet into a fancy pair of high-heeled shoes. Adding a hat and a matching purse draped over my shoulder, I looked smart. Now, as their speaker, I paraded my confidence and self-assured womanhood. After the hilarious laughter! The message of how deceived we can be when putting our worth in outward fashion has begun to soak into us as women.

At this moment, I am looking at the style section of today's, October 11, paper. Underneath a big picture of a pair of 5" heels is the caption, "Blue metallic cage heels by Jimmy Choo for H&M cost $129 in 2009, but now sell for around $270.00. Designer name items from Target are re-selling for $100 to $200 higher." We want it, we think we need it; and it is working! In Satan's world, attractiveness, pride, money, and power are indeed to be expected, so who is Satan using his disguise on? _____

_____

How is he disguising himself? _____

As believing women of this century, the words "submit" and "authority" create animosity and rebellion. Why? _____

_____

Has submission often been taught only in regard to women? That is not what the Scripture teaches. I submit (willingly) to my husband in response to his love for me as Christ's example. Each believer is to submit (willingly) to each other in response to Christ's love for His body, the Church. Mutual submission is the work of the cross! Fruit of the Spirit is the evidence.

Jesus told His disciples it is through authority, domination, and oppression that the sinful world operates, but this is not how He intended His followers to live. He came to serve, even washing their feet. He told His disciples to go out and do what He had done.

Read Matthew 20:24-28; 23:11; Mark 9:34; Luke 9:46; 22:24.

Is this our day of worth? _____

Are we not to feel good about ourselves? _____

Don't we deserve to be equal? _____

Is it wrong for women to be praised? _____

Christ, our Messiah, answered those questions. He is looking for women willing to stand and speak His truth in love for the edification of His body under His will and power. Many witnesses have gone before us and paid a great price to clear the path. We, too, must put on the whole armor and join them for the benefit of future generations.

Nonetheless, we are also at a very dangerous crossroad and turning point. Remember, Eve had everything and was convinced Satan's worth was more desirable than God's worth. I must always be aware that I can take pride in womanhood and be captured by the subtlety of the angel of light.

Read carefully Ephesians 4:11-17, and become the part that supplies health to a strong body for spiritual growth!

Are you touched by an angel of light or redeemed by a crucified Lord?

PROMISE

Whosoever exalts himself shall be humbled;

And whosoever humbles himself

Shall be exalted.

—Matthew 23:12 NASB

PRAYER

Heavenly Father, I thank you that I have been created in your image and my worth has been paid for by the blood of your Son, Jesus. Help me to rely on Your strength, wisdom, and power and not on myself. I submit my will and my desires, present and future, to be used for Your glory. Amen.

Part 5
Accepting and Finding Your Worth

All One In Christ

If God be for us, who can be against us?
—Romans 8:31a KJV

If we believe we are created in the image of God, followers of Jesus, Yeshua, the Son of God, members of the body of Christ yet restrict ourselves because we are women, we are misrepresenting the all-powerful, all-loving, all-knowing God we serve. If that be the case, all the great sermons preached over the years by men would have to attach an addendum stating, "Only men can apply for full benefits." Jon Zens states in What's Wrong with Paul and Women, "Thus, to use I Timothy 2:11-15 as a basis to completely silence the sisters in Christian assemblies is hardly an accurate way to handle Scripture. It uses one context to cancel out the revelation of many others."

Read and discuss the following women from Scripture who affirm God the Father, Christ, and the Holy Spirit is the author of diversity, equality, and justice, and all His creation was created for His pleasure (Jeremiah 9:23, 24).

1. *Sarah:* A great influence on her family and marriage. She becomes the mother of a promised miracle son in her nineties. Genesis 11 and 12.

2. *Hagar:* A slave owned and controlled by the household of Abraham. Despised and sent away homeless, she becomes the first women to be spoken to by God through his messenger. Genesis 16.

3. *Puah* and *Shiphrah:* Two Hebrew women put in charge of all of Egyptians midwives and feared God more than the king. Exodus 1:15-22.

4. *Deborah:* A judge, prophetess, and military leader who led Israel into a victorious battle, yet willing to give another woman (Jael) the honor. Judges 4.

5. *Rahab:* Referred to in Scripture as a "harlot." She heard about the great God of the Israelites and chose to follow Him. She saved her family and was given a place in the genealogy of Christ.

6. *Ruth:* A young widow who became a refugee of sorts, living in a country with no ancestors, yet her son was the grandfather of King David, an ancestor to Jesus, the Messiah of Israel. A book was also named in her honor.

7. *Leah* and *Rachel:* They built the house of Israel. Quite a legacy. Ruth 4:11.

8. *Huldah:* A prophetess and wife, who carried out both duties quite well. King Josiah sent his priest to inquire of her about the words found in the book of the law. 2 Kings 22.

9. *Esther:* An orphan girl under God's providence who becomes a queen. She saves her people from complete annihilation. A book and holiday feast are in her honor.

10. *Elizabeth* and *Mary* we have already studied.

11. *Anna:* An elderly widow, also referred to as a prophetess, was privileged to recognize Mary's baby and proclaim Him "to all those that looked for redemption in Jerusalem." Luke 2:37-38.

12. *The Samaritian Woman:* A divorcee who became a great preacher with many souls to her credit. John 4.

13. *Dorcas:* A seamstress and caregiver full of good works. She became a pillar in the early church and was called a disciple. Acts 9.

14. *Mary Magdalene:* Possessed by seven demons before meeting Christ, she became—along with Mary, the mother of Jesus—one of the most mentioned women in the New Testament. She was also a disciple and financial supporter of Jesus' ministry. Recorded in all the Gospels.

15. *Mary* and *Martha:* Unmarried sisters, one sat at the feet of Jesus to learn (breaking Jewish custom), while the other found her place in the kitchen. They were very close friends of Christ, and He spent time in their home.

No other religion shows the equality, diversity, or love of women like the God of Abraham, Isaac, and Jacob through the sacrifice of Jesus, His only Son, by the power of the Holy Spirit! Sparrows, ravens, and lilies are cared for so not one slips away from God's watchful or loving hand. yet He says how much more your are valued!

Jesus came to speak and show us the very character of His Father, telling us "That you may be the children of your Father which is in heaven: he makes his sun to rise on the evil and on the good, and sends rain on the just and on the unjust" (Matthew 5:45). Also in Matthew 22:16, I read that as the Pharisees were trying to trip up Christ, they said, "Teacher, we know you are a man of integrity [truthful] and that you teach the way of God in accordance with the truth. You are not swayed [care not, KJV] by men, because you pay no attention to who they are."

This is the God we serve: "no respect of persons." My God, my Redeemer, is not concerned about wealth, education, gender, or family name. He is concerned only about the condition, love, and belief in my heart in the Son He sent to give us eternal life.

Place your name in the Scripture and ask yourself if God has limited you because you are a woman.

Pray a prayer of dedication, and add your name to the list of women to be used by God to carry out His plan and exalt His Son.

Let us remind ourselves of the words God spoke to Elizabeth and Mary: "For with God nothing shall be impossible"

PROMISE

Blessed are they that do his commandments,
That they may have right to the tree of life, and may
enter through the gates into the city.
Revelation 22:14 KJV

PRAYER

To be used of God to speak, to sing, to pray,
To be used of God to show someone the way,
To be used of God, that is my desire.

Conclusion

*Thou shall love the Lord thy God, with all thy heart,
and with all thy soul, and with all thy mind.
—Matthew 22:37 (KJV)*

My father was a handsome, strong minister all his life. But one night changed all that. Although he had experienced a previous heart attack, he was back on his feet doing what he loved most, preaching.

This call that came in the middle of the night was different. "Come quickly! Something is wrong with Dad!" As we entered the room, it was evident he had a stroke. His speech was no longer clear, yet he thought he was still in control. He would try to sit up on the side of the bed, but if we did not hold him, this strong man would simply fall over. One side of his body had been paralyzed. It was a heartbreaking an painful scene I know many families have experienced.

My father could no longer be the man who stood strong in the pulpit, declaring the good news. The reality is that we all live in an earthly body that grows old, but, that good news he preached all his life promises a new body and living eternally with our Lord! What a hope!

With each stroke, my father's body became more incapacitated and dependent. My mother chose to keep him at home rather than placing him in a nursing facility, which the doctor recommended. He spent his last days on a hospital bed in their dining room. I was the one staying with them during those very difficult days. One Sunday afternoon, after sitting in silence, she went over to the piano and began to play his favorite hymns, and we did our best to sing along.

The last voluntary movement I ever saw my father make was to raise one arm as far as he could in praise to his God while my mother played. It was his last motion of independence. The images I don't like to recall are of his body becoming increasingly debilitated. It is overwhelming, heartbreaking, and painful to know you are helpless.

As I experienced this paralyzing of my father's physical body, I couldn't help but compare it with Christ's spiritual body. Christ being our spiritual head, full of all power, all knowledge, all wisdom and waiting to live within us making his body, the church, complete in him Yet, there remains teachings that one half cannot function fully to the capacity of our spiritual head.

How paralyzing, heartbreaking, and restraining this must be to our Redeemer, who has been given all power in heaven and on earth. It is the Head—Christ—that controls the body, not the other way around.

Have we been deceived? _____

In this twenty-first century, Christian religious organizations have experienced wealth and growth that has not been seen in previous years. Yet, the resistance is still present to embrace equality and diversity in the body of Christ.

But speaking the truth in love, [we] may grow up into him in all things, which is the head, even Christ: From whom the *whole body* fitly joined *together* and *compacted* by that which every *joint supplies,* according to the effectual working in the *measure of every part,* makes increase of the *body* unto the edifying of itself in *love.* (Ephesians 4:15, 16 KJV); emphases added)

Jesus also gives us His picture of equality in Matthew 12:46-50 (KJV). The house was crowded with people eager to hear Christ's teachings. He was told His mother and brothers were outside, waiting to speak to Him. He quickly responded, asking, "Who is my mother, and who are my brothers?" He answered His own question by pointing to His followers. "These are my family. For whosoever shall do the will of my Father which is in heaven, the same is my brother, and sister and mother."

Pray for unity to experience fully Acts 2:16-18! Seek the face of Christ through His Word. Meditate and surrender your *all* to His *love*. Then take your place of value in His Body to be used for His glory and His kingdom!

"So God created man in his image, in the image of God created he him; male and female created he them. And God blessed them."

PROMISE

For God so love the world, that he gave his only begotten Son, that whosoever believes in him should not perish, but have everlasting life.

—John 3:16 KJV

PRAYER

Write down your prayer of faith.

Questions for Discussion

1. When standing before God Almighty in judgment, what will be the key to entering His kingdom?

2. Do you believe your gender will be an excuse for not doing God's will? How does gender fit into Matthew 7:21-23?

3. If your church discriminates against women in equality of service, how would it explain Jesus' answer in Matthew 22:29-32?

4. Does outward appearance or gender supersede faith and surrender? See 1 Samuel 16:7; John 7:24; 2 Corinthians 10:7.

5. Is the Bible used, misused, or misinterpreted in your church to limit the calling or gifting of women to ministry? Why?

6. Explain the difference between secular feminist movements and biblical equality.

7. Do you know women who have experienced gender bias by the church?

8. How can you or the church, (body of Christ) heal the wounds of many hurting women and bring them back into full productivity for Christ?

9. In one word, what is the key to worth and holiness for Gentiles/Jews, males/females? See Romans 11:20 and Galatians 3:26-29.

Bibliography

Alexander, Estrelda, and Amos Yong. *Philip's Daughters.* Eugene, Ore.: Pickwick Publications, 2009.

Belleville, Linda L. *Women Leaders and the Church: 3 Crucial Questions.* Grand Rapids, Mich.: Baker Book House, 2000.

Bristow, John Temple. *What Paul Really Said about Women.* San Francisco: Harper San Francisco, 1991.

George, Janet. *Still Side by Side.* Minneapolis: Christians for Biblical Equality, 2009.

Grady, J. Lee. *10 Lies the Church Tells Women.* Lake Mary, Fla.: Charisma House, 2000.

Grady, J. Lee. *25 Tough Questions about Women and the Church.* Lake Mary, Fla.: Charisma House, 2003.

Hales, Thomas. *The Applied Old Testament Commentary: Applying God's Word to Your Life.* Colorado Springs: David C. Cook, 2007f

Heatherley, Joyce Landorf. *The Fragrance of Beauty.* (20th printing 1980) Wheaton, Ill.: Victor Books, 1991.

Jantz, Gregory L. Healing the Scars of Emotional Abuse. Grand Rapids, Mich.: Fleming H. Revell, 1995.

Mother Teresa. *Heart of Joy.* Bloomington, Minn.: Garborg's Publishers, 2001.

Mother Teresa. *12,000 Religious Quotations.* Grand Rapids, Mich.: Baker Book House, 1989.

Price, Eugenia. *Discoveries.* Grand Rapids, Mich.: Zondervan, 1955.

Richards, Sue, and Larry Richards. *Every Woman in the Bible.* Nashville: Nelson Publishers, Thomas, 1999.

Rosewell, Pam. *Not I, but Christ.* Nashville: Nelson Publishers, Thomas, 1984.

Wilcox, Carolyn L. *Snakes in the Pulpit: Hope for Victims of Deception.* Lake Mary, Fla.: Creation House, 2010.

Zens, Jon. *What's with Paul and Women.* Omaha: Ekklesia Press, 2010.